APR 2017

DISCARD
FCPL discards materials that are outdated and in poor condition. In order to make room for current, in-demand materials, underused materials are offered for public sale.

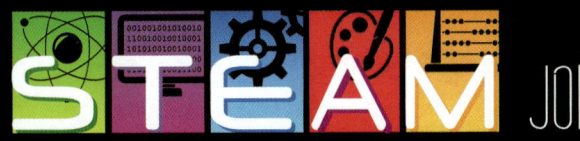

Rec

STEAM JOBS IN

Photography

Ray Reyes

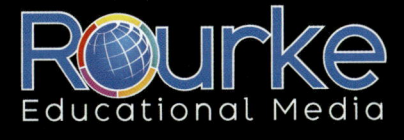

Rourke Educational Media

rourkeeducationalmedia.com

Scan for Related Titles and Teacher Resources

Before & After Reading Activities

Level: U

Before Reading:

Building Academic Vocabulary and Background Knowledge

Before reading a book, it is important to tap into what your child or students already know about the topic. This will help them develop their vocabulary, increase their reading comprehension, and make connections across the curriculum.

1. Look at the cover of the book. What will this book be about?
2. What do you already know about the topic?
3. Let's study the Table of Contents. What will you learn about in the book's chapters?
4. What would you like to learn about this topic? Do you think you might learn about it from this book? Why or why not?
5. Use a reading journal to write about your knowledge of this topic. Record what you already know about the topic and what you hope to learn about the topic.
6. Read the book.
7. In your reading journal, record what you learned about the topic and your response to the book.
8. After reading the book complete the activities below.

Content Area Vocabulary
Read the list. What do these words mean?

aperture
calibrates
celestial
contrast
diffuse
elements
exposure
increments
optics
resolution
sensitivity
sensor
shutter
telephoto
wavelengths

After Reading:

Comprehension and Extension Activity

After reading the book, work on the following questions with your child or students in order to check their level of reading comprehension and content mastery.

1. What part does a cinematographer play in the making of a movie? (Summarize)
2. What kind of sensors do modern cameras have and what does each one do? (Inferring)
3. What year was the oldest surviving photograph taken? (Asking questions)
4. What does the camera on the Kepler Space Telescope measure? (Text to self connection)
5. What guideline do all photographers use? (Asking questions)

Extension Activity

Grab a camera or your phone and pick a starting location. Take 100 steps in any direction. When you get to 100, stop. Compose and frame a photo from where you are standing. See where your steps take you and what you can create!

Table of Contents

What is STEAM?. 4
Commercial Photography 11
Adventures in Astrophotography 18
Engineering Photo Equipment. 24
Lights, Camera, Action 30
Making Photos Better and Brighter 36
Advancing Photography with STEAM 42
STEAM Job Facts 44
Glossary 46
Index 47
Show What You Know 47
Websites to Visit 47
About the Author 48

What is STEAM?

A photojournalist roams the sideline at a football game and snaps a picture of the game-winning touchdown. A cinematographer studies a movie set to determine the best angles for lighting the actors and the scene. An engineer designs special lenses that produce breathtaking images of outer space.

These people all have jobs that require knowledge of photography. And each one learned the principles of photography with a STEAM education. STEAM is a quick way to talk about the fields of science, technology, engineering, art, and mathematics. Photography records light to create lasting images. It applies all aspects of STEAM to make that possible.

STEAM Fast Fact:

Photography is the process of catching light. It comes from the Greek words *phos* and *photo*, which mean *light*, and *graphe*, which means drawing. So when you take photographs, you're drawing with light!

Take the Shot

Flip through a magazine and take a close look at its photographs. If you're reading a nature or wildlife magazine, you'll find pictures of exotic animals and stunning landscapes. If you're looking through a sports magazine, you'll see photos of basketball players frozen in midair for a slam dunk, or baseball outfielders stretching out their bodies to snag a ball.

Photojournalists travel to these locations to tell stories for readers. Sometimes they take images that record history, such as newly elected U.S. presidents taking an oath before they start work in the Oval Office. Photojournalists capture events and scenery from all over the world and send them to magazines and websites for publication.

Photojournalists know they only have a few seconds to take a picture of an important moment. They quickly make calculations before even composing the shot. Photographers adjust camera settings to account for several factors such as: the **aperture** of their lens, the speed of the camera's **shutter**, and the **sensitivity** of the camera's **sensor** to light. All three together determine **exposure**, which ensures the photo is not too dark or too bright.

Today's cameras have easy-to-read displays that show information like shutter speed and aperture to help photographers select the correct exposure.

STEAM in Action!

A photographer adjusts their camera's aperture setting to control how much light enters the lens. The aperture of a lens has a lot in common with the pupil of the human eye! And you can watch how your pupils change depending on the light.

Take a magnifying glass and put it on a handheld mirror. Hold it close to your face until you see your eyes focused and enlarged in the magnifying glass. Now use a small flashlight and shine it directly into the pupil of your eye. What do you see? Bounce the flashlight off the mirror. What changed?

Go into a dim room. Close one eye and look into your open eye. What's the difference in your pupil in the dark room compared to when you pointed the flashlight into your eye?

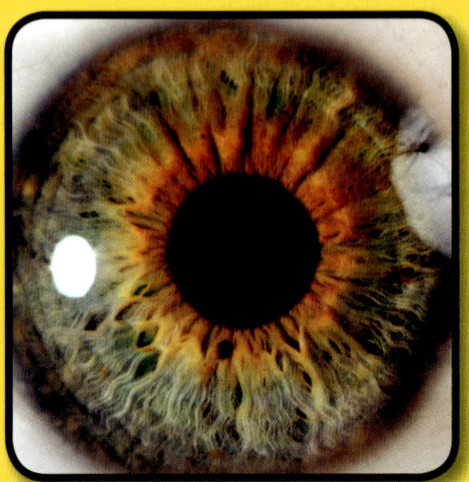
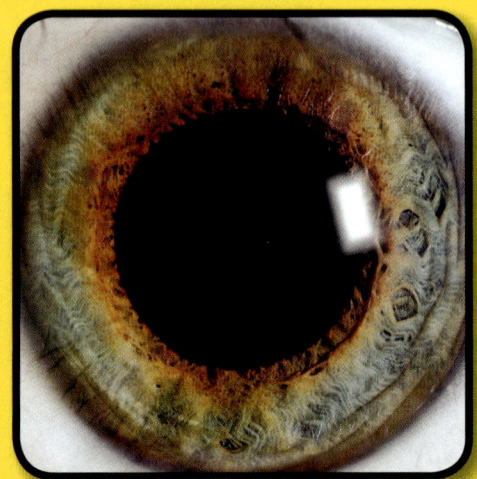

The pupil of your eye is similar to the aperture of a camera lens, shrinking and opening depending on the brightness of light.

Photojournalists can also get creative with camera settings to freeze action or slow it down to show motion. Photographers use math to get the settings just right. Controlling shutter speed employs fractions. For example, setting a camera's speed to 1/100 means the shutter opens and closes in one-one hundredth of a second. That's fast! That shutter speed can take a landscape photo showing puffy clouds overhead.

When a photographer wants to illustrate motion, the camera's shutter speed settings are slowed in one-half or one-third **increments**. Cameras can actually keep their shutters open for 30 seconds or longer. A shutter speed set for that long will show those puffy clouds moving across the sky!

STEAM Fast Fact:

Modern digital cameras have shutter speeds that go as fast as 1/8,000 of a second. That's so fast, you can take a picture of a drop of water floating in midair!

Real STEAM Job: *Photojournalist*

Photojournalists travel all over the world documenting important events, people, and moments. Like all photographers, photojournalists have a scientific understanding of the principles of light. They know how to control it through their camera settings, which uses numbers in one-half or one-third increments to adjust a photograph's exposure.

This job requires math skills. Photojournalists also need strong computer skills to tone and adjust photos before sending them to newspapers, magazines, or websites.

A photojournalist's work is not finished after he or she stops shooting. Photojournalists also tone digital photos for magazines and newspapers.

Commercial Photography

A new restaurant just opened. The owners want to create a website to show customers what the restaurant looks like and the food it serves. They hire a commercial photographer to take pictures of the restaurant and the items on the menu.

Commercial photography covers a broad range of subjects, such as jewelry, clothing, houses, and food. Commercial photographers specialize in photos that show off the merchandise and services that companies sell.

Food photographers use props like a recipe's ingredients to enhance a product's look. Doesn't this pizza look delicious?

Commercial photographers take photos of products, such as soft drinks and vehicles, that are seen on billboards. They also take pictures of the toys and electronics you find in print advertisements and on store websites.

While photojournalists only have a few seconds to take an important picture, commercial photographers have more time. They can set up different backgrounds and additional lighting equipment to get the perfect shot.

This studio lighting setup ensures that the model is well lit from every angle and that no distracting shadows fall across her face or body.

Light is a form of energy that travels in waves. Commercial photographers know how to harness and control that energy to make a company's product truly shine. With the proper equipment, commercial photographers can bend, bounce, and **diffuse** light around a subject. The photographer then decides the best composition and angle for the image.

These techniques can cast a shadow or a spotlight on a product, creating a mood for people looking at the advertisement.

Special colored filters and lighting can give commercial photographs a sleek, edgy look.

STEAM Fast Fact:

Light travels at about 670 million miles (180 million kilometers) per hour. At that speed, it takes about eight minutes for the sun's light to reach Earth.

STEAM in Action!

All photographers use a guideline known as the rule of thirds to compose photos. When it's followed, the rule helps photographers create an image that is more pleasing to the eye.

The rule breaks down an image into nine sections using two imaginary vertical lines and two horizontal lines. The lines form a grid. A photographer places the subject he wants to shoot in the areas where the lines intersect.

You can see how the rule works with a smartphone. Open the smartphone's camera app and imagine the nine-part grid on your phone. If the app you're using has the option of turning on the grid, go ahead and use that!

Go outside and take a picture of a single object, like a flower, tree, or street sign. Place the object directly in the center of the frame and take the photo. How does it look?

Now use the rule of thirds and take a photo of the same object at any point where the lines of the grid cross. How does the photo look now? Is it more visually interesting than the first picture you took?

Some commercial photographers work with the latest technology to get images taken from an amazing perspective. Real estate photographers use drones to snap pictures of houses and buildings from high above. No matter what equipment or software they use, photographers never forget the rule of thirds.

STEAM Fast Fact:

The 18th century engraver John Thomas Smith was the first person to write down the rule of thirds. The guideline is also used in design, painting, and movies.

Real STEAM Job: *Product Photographer*

Manufacturers of well-known brands of shoes, electronics, and clothing need images of their products for advertising. That's the job of the product photographer.

Companies like Microsoft, Nike, Chevrolet, and Sony hire product photographers to create images of their latest gadgets and models. The product photographer needs to understand how the companies want to showcase the products for consumers.

Photographers select location and lighting to capture the look and feel of a company's product.

People specializing in product photography get creative with light, angles, and props to make the products stand out from all the other brands. They need a strong understanding of the properties of light. Some even develop graphic design skills to further enhance the look of the products they shoot. Others work with the latest photography equipment such as aerial drones and GoPro video cameras.

Drone cameras can capture stunning overhead views of buildings and landscapes.

Graphic design is an important skill for product photographers. It lets them make products more appealing to consumers.

Adventures in Astrophotography

Photographers travel the globe. Astrophotographers go farther. People specializing in astrophotography create images of craters on the moon, sand dunes on Mars, and mountains on Pluto! Astrophotographers help increase our knowledge of the universe.

Astrophotographers are scientists. They work in universities and observatories. Some work for private companies that partner with NASA (National Aeronautics and Space Administration) to take images shared with the general public.

icy mountains on Pluto

red, sandy surface of Mars

Astrophotographers employ highly specialized lenses, telescopes, and computer programs. They use this equipment to observe **celestial** objects in the night sky. They record data such as the types of **elements** found in stars.

The universe is vast and mysterious. That's why astrophotographers also work with cameras that record images in **wavelengths** of light and energy invisible to human eyes! This technique helps us piece together the birth of stars and the origins of the universe.

Mauna Kea Observatories, Hawaii

STEAM Fast Fact:

Invisible wavelengths are infrared, ultraviolet, x-rays and gamma rays. Infrared is heat. Ultraviolet comes from the sun and causes a suntan or a sunburn. X-rays take pictures of your bones. Gamma radiation is generated in nuclear reactions.

STEAM in Action!

The light we see from sunlight or moonlight appears to have no color. But think about rainbows. They appear when sunlight is reflected through water or ice in the atmosphere. The different colors you see are the visible light spectrum.

You can take a closer look at the visible light spectrum by using a prism or a garden hose. Shine a light through the prism using a flashlight or sunlight streaming through a window. Turn the prism until you see a rainbow appear on a white wall or blank piece of paper.

If you're using a garden hose, put your thumb over the nozzle until the water sprays. Stand with the sun at your back. Turn slowly until you see a rainbow! There are six colors in the visible light spectrum. Did you see them all? What are the colors?

On July 14, 2015, the *New Horizons* spacecraft made its closest approach to Pluto. The piano-sized spaceship took hundreds of photos of the dwarf planet with specialized **telephoto** cameras from thousands of miles away. *New Horizons* then began transmitting the images back to Earth.

Scientists and imaging specialists at NASA studied the data. They downloaded the photos and developed photographs of Pluto to share with the world.

The camera on the *New Horizons* spacecraft took photos of Pluto's ice mountains and frozen plains from as far as 1 million miles (1.6 million kilometers) away.

Pluto is 4.6 million miles (7.4 million kilometers) away. Astrophotography, astronomy, and photography helped make this impressive feat of engineering possible!

Real STEAM Job: *NASA Imaging Specialist*

Rovers crawl the surface of Mars. Spacecraft zoom around the moons of Saturn. The Hubble Space Telescope peers at distant galaxies. This fleet of robotic explorers all take photographs and send them back to Earth.

Some photos are black and white. Other images are taken in different wavelengths. Imaging specialists analyze the data and use the information to add accurate colors. Every NASA photo you've seen of planets and stars that made you say "Wow!" were developed by imaging specialists with a strong grasp of photography and science.

Mars *Curiosity* rover

The images increase our understanding of the universe. Imaging specialists at NASA share the wonders of the cosmos with everyone on Earth.

Kepler Space Telescope

STEAM Fast Fact:

The Kepler Space Telescope launched in 2009 on a mission to find planets outside of our solar system. It has a special camera that only measures the intensity of light. Kepler discovered more than 1,000 new worlds orbiting other stars!

Engineering Photo Equipment

Professional photographers can't do their jobs without cameras and lenses. Technology improves fast. Photographers need the newest gear to replace outdated or worn equipment.

Today's cameras are far more advanced than cameras built ten years ago. And those decade-old cameras were technological marvels compared to the film and Polaroid cameras that came before. Engineers design and build the equipment that keeps photographers on the cutting edge of technology.

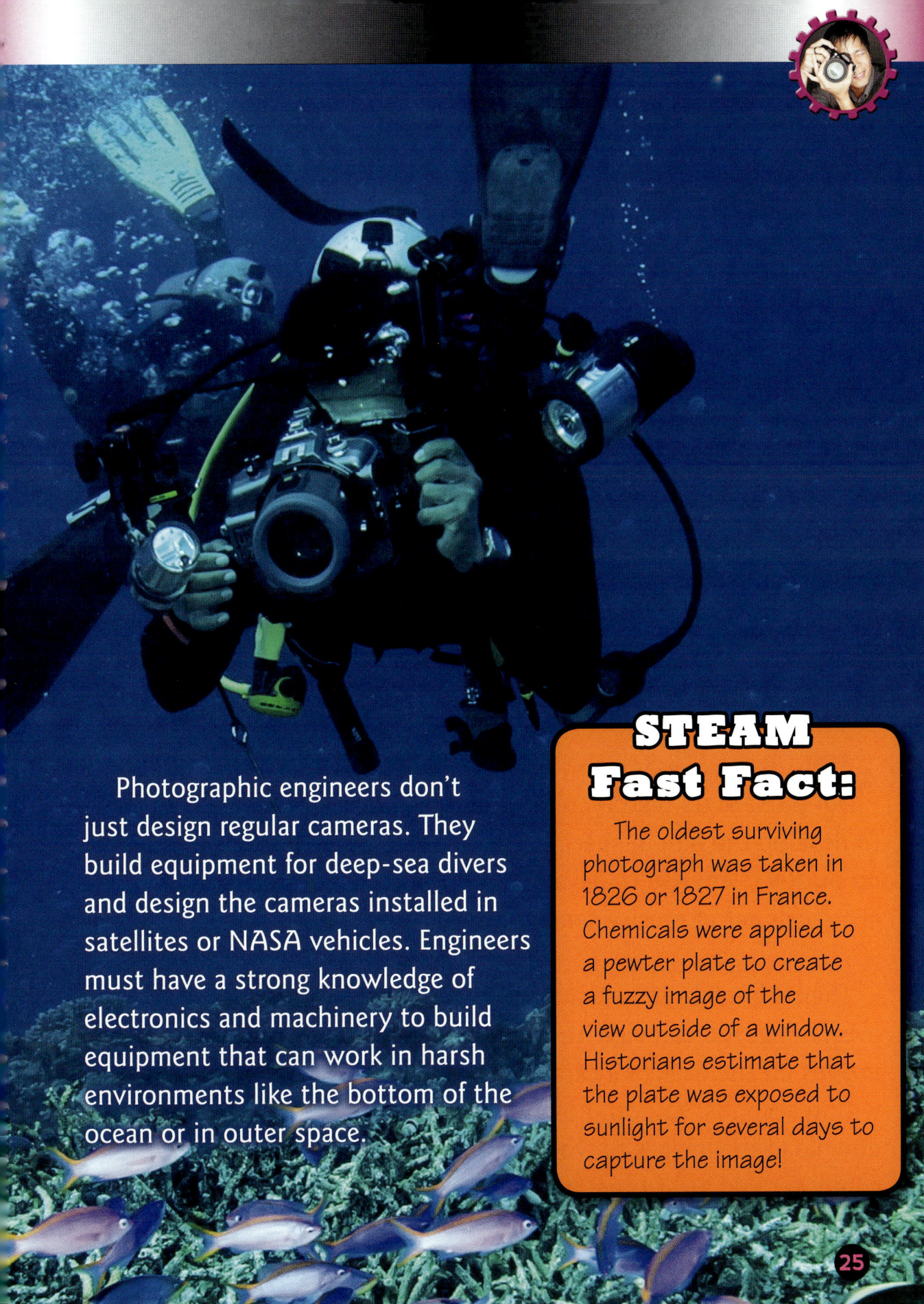

Photographic engineers don't just design regular cameras. They build equipment for deep-sea divers and design the cameras installed in satellites or NASA vehicles. Engineers must have a strong knowledge of electronics and machinery to build equipment that can work in harsh environments like the bottom of the ocean or in outer space.

STEAM Fast Fact:

The oldest surviving photograph was taken in 1826 or 1827 in France. Chemicals were applied to a pewter plate to create a fuzzy image of the view outside of a window. Historians estimate that the plate was exposed to sunlight for several days to capture the image!

Before cameras went digital, photographs were developed in dark rooms with special lighting and chemicals.

Building High-Tech Gear

For most of its history, photography relied on film. It took hours to develop the film in special rooms. There were no computers and no printers. You had to develop and print the pictures with special chemicals set at precise temperatures.

Digital photography changed everything. You can view the images on the back of a camera within seconds. You can now download the images on your computer and print them in a few minutes.

That's the work of photographic engineers! They find ways to improve and enhance equipment. They design lenses that work in the rain or freezing weather. Without engineers, photographers wouldn't be able to take their equipment to the remote locations and challenging climates that their work requires.

Light goes through a camera's lens and shutter, recording an image on the digital sensor, which is then saved to the camera's memory card.

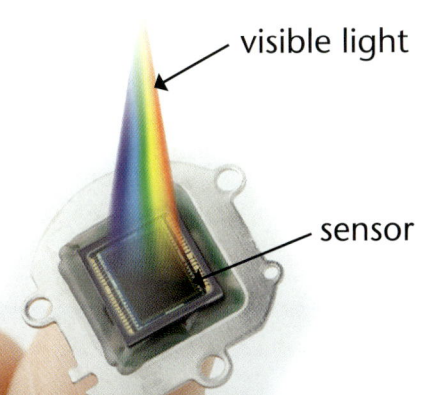

visible light

sensor

Engineers also work to improve the sensors of modern cameras. Digital sensors replaced film. Images are recorded on an electronic sensor, then transmitted to the camera's memory card. The **resolution** of today's cameras is so sharp and clear, photos can be taken in almost complete darkness.

STEAM in Action!

Modern camera sensors come in two sizes: full frame or cropped. A full frame sensor has a wide angle of view.

Cropped sensors have a smaller angle of view. Although cropped sensors are smaller than full frame, they can actually take photos of distant objects better than full frame cameras.

full frame sensor

cropped sensor

Here's how. If you put a 35 millimeter (mm) lens on a full frame camera, the image you see through the viewfinder displays a whole room. If you put a 35mm lens on a cropped sensor camera, the sides and walls of the room appear cropped, or cut out. Why?

Real STEAM Job: *Photographic Engineer*

Photographic engineers must have a strong knowledge of electronics. They understand the principles of **optics**. Some have knowledge in chemistry, which allows them to make special scratch-proof coatings for lenses.

They have strong backgrounds in mechanical engineering, which helps them build the shutters and mirrors in cameras. Some are materials scientists; they choose materials such as metals and plastic alloys to make cameras lighter and tougher. They test cameras to make sure they last for many years in all kinds of weather.

Photographic engineers also build the computer processors in cameras. Others are computer programmers who design the software that controls a camera's autofocus features and powers a camera's menu.

Cropped sensors are measured by what's known as a multiplier. The multiplier in most Canon camera sensors is 1.6x. So if you use a 35mm lens on a cropped sensor and multiply it by 1.6, you actually get a closer field of view and a narrower focal length of 56mm. That means you can stand farther away from the subject you want to photograph!

What happens when you put a 50mm lens on a camera with a cropped sensor multiplier of 1.6x? What happens when you put a 200mm lens on a camera with a cropped sensor multiplier of 1.3x?

Lights, Camera, Action

Watching movies with your family and friends and a big tub of popcorn guarantees a great time. Movies evoke emotion. They thrill you, make you think, and make you laugh.

Of course, your favorite actors play a large role. But the people working behind the camera are also important. The director of photography, also called a cinematographer, is one of the key jobs on a movie set. A cinematographer is basically a movie's photographer.

Cinematographers know the basic principles of photography. They understand composition, lighting, and shadow to control mood. Cinematographers are skilled with placing actors within a frame to attract an audience's attention to important events in the plot. The director of photography works with the movie director to select the kind of lenses they want to use for every shot.

Cinematographers, or directors of photography, operate the camera for motion picture productions. They compose, plan, and coordinate each filming sequence.

STEAM in Action!

Watch one of your favorite movies at home. Study the opening scene in the movie, the shot where a character is introduced or the place where the movie is set.

How did the cinematographer frame the shot? Was the rule of thirds used? Was the character in the center of the frame?

Look at a scene shot during the day. How bright is it? Where is the sun? Watch a scene at night. Are there any lights shining on the actors? What direction is it coming from? What color are the lights? How does the lighting used in these scenes make you feel?

Movie cameras are mounted on cranes, tracks, or even harnessed to camera operators so that they can follow actors' movements.

The director of photography also decides the movie's look and mood. Will it be shot with film or with digital cameras? Color or black and white? Will the camera move with the actors or stay in place?

Cinematographers on animated films also work closely with computer animators to design the lighting, colors, and composition for the movie's scenes. The lighting animator then takes the cinematographer's direction and applies light and shadow to characters and backgrounds.

Real STEAM Job: *Lighting Artist*

Lighting artists work on computer-generated characters and special effects. They have training in 3-D art, computer software, and programming. They also have knowledge about the qualities of light, like color and angle. Lighting artists make computer-animated water look like real water. They understand how light reflects and scatters.

Lighting artists also have experience with cinematography. They know how lighting is used on movie sets and copy that look on a computer. They use software to make the lighting in an animated movie feel real and natural. Some lighting artists have college degrees in computer animation, art, or theater.

STEAM Fast Fact:

Most modern digital cameras record video. Cinematographers have used cameras you can buy in the store to shoot several scenes from big Hollywood films! These movies include: Captain America, Thor, and The Avengers.

Making Photos Better and Brighter

Photographers who use digital cameras have many high-tech tools at their disposal that make their photographs look brighter, sharper, and more colorful.

Most photographers edit their own photos. They use computer software to crop and rotate images. They increase or decrease the saturation, exposure, and **contrast** of an image. They can apply digital filters to make photos appear like they were taken with a film or Polaroid camera. They can turn a color image into a black and white photo.

Computer programmers and app developers create the software that photographers use to enhance photographs. Some companies just focus on making software that **calibrates** computer monitors to display the most accurate color possible.

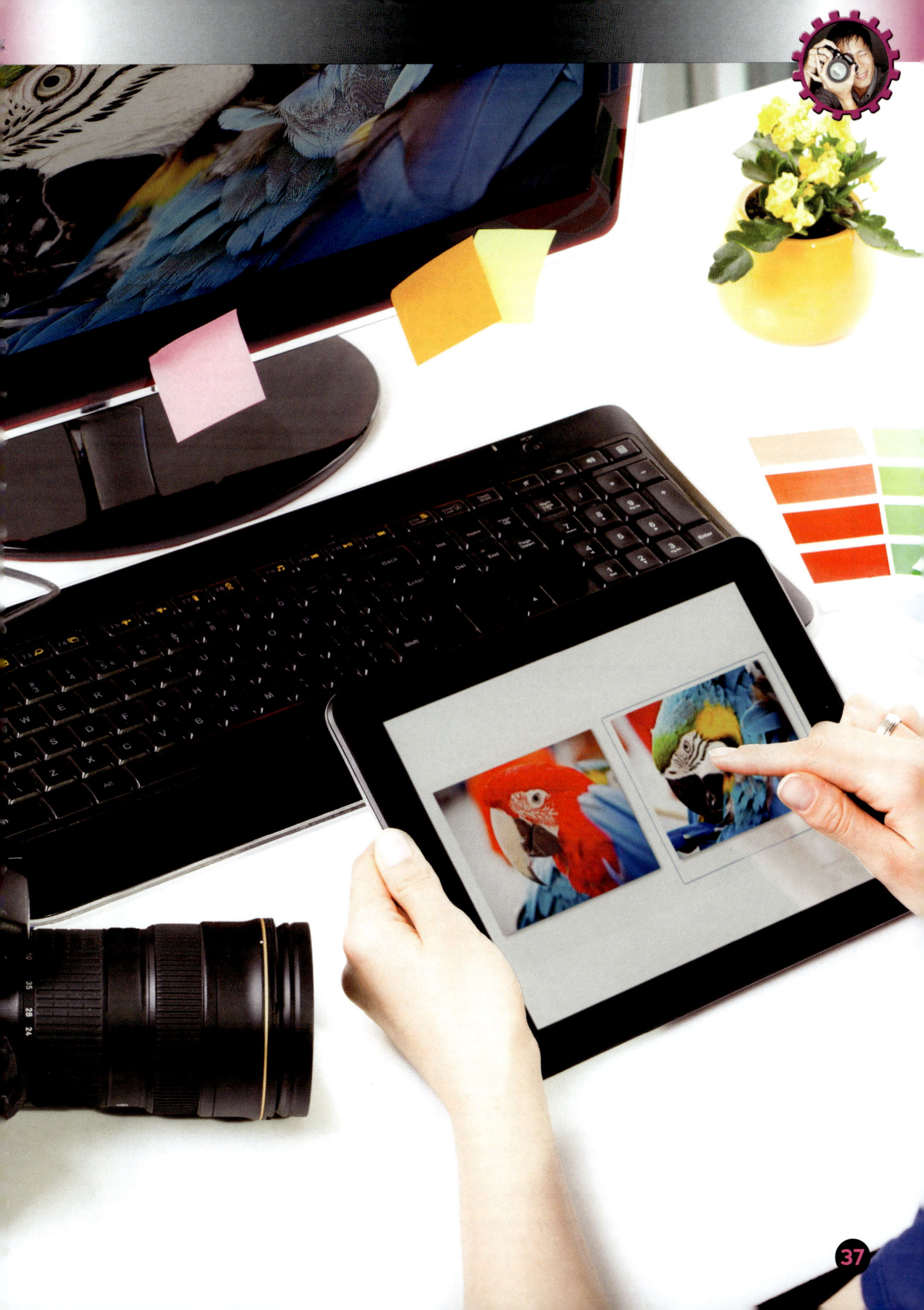

STEAM in Action!

Computer software helps photographers enhance images. The most common photo editing software is found on smartphones.

Open the photo app on a smartphone and take a picture. Next, press the edit button. You'll find more buttons or sliders that lets you adjust your picture's color, tone, and contrast. Try it!

You may also find a button for different filters. The filters imitate how photos used to look when they were taken with film. Choose a filter that appeals to you. You've now edited a picture like a professional photographer.

Photographers also use special hardware to edit photos. Hardware designers construct special tablets and electronic pens that photographers can use instead of a mouse to edit images. Electronics companies make high-definition computer monitors with photographers and cinematographers in mind.

Photographers know that in the digital age, having just a camera is not enough. They employ a wide array of high-tech tools to bring their artistic vision to life.

Who needs a mouse? Some photographers use electronic tablets and pens to edit, tone, and color photos.

Real STEAM Job: *Photographic Software Developer*

Photography is closely tied to technology. Advances in computer software and programming help photographers do their jobs quickly and creatively.

Software engineers design programs that enhance photographs. They are trained in the basic principles of photography and know what photographers need.

Photographic software developers are expert computer coders. They apply computer science, engineering, and math to design, develop, and test software.

Software engineers design features that allow photographers to edit photos directly in a camera. Engineers also create programs that run on desktop computers, tablets, and smartphones. They help photographers develop photos for the whole world to see and enjoy!

The many photo apps you see on computers, tablets, and smartphones were designed by software engineers.

Advancing Photography with STEAM

Photography combines technology and art. A photographer's vision and creativity is expressed through high-tech lenses, cameras, and computer software. People with STEAM knowledge are important to the advancement of photography because the technology in this field is always improving and growing.

By doing research, asking questions, and solving problems, STEAM workers in photography can capture or help create timeless images of the world around us.

STEAM Job Facts

Photojournalist
Important Skills: mathematics, science, logistic problem-solving, critical thinking
Important Knowledge: mathematics, computers
College Major: photography or photojournalism

Commercial Photographer
Important Skills: mathematics, science, logistic problem-solving, critical thinking, active listening
Important Knowledge: mathematics, computers, advertising, marketing
College Major: fine art photography or photojournalism

NASA Imaging Specialist
Important Skills: mathematics, physics, astronomy, critical thinking
Important Knowledge: computers, mechanics, engineering, design
College Major: astronomy or physics

Photographic Engineer

Important Skills: mathematics, critical thinking, science, complex problem-solving

Important Knowledge: engineering and technology, design, mechanics, mathematics, electronics

College Major: mechanical or electrical engineering

Lighting Artist

Important Skills: mathematics, science, computer science, art

Important Knowledge: photography, computers, cinematography, design theory, color theory

College Major: computer animation or computer design

Software Engineer

Important Skills: complex problem-solving, programming, systems analysis, judgement and decision making

Important Knowledge: computers, electronics, mathematics, English, engineering

College Major: computer engineering or computer programming

Glossary

aperture (AP-er-cher): an opening in a lens that admits light

calibrates (KAL-uh-breyts): to determine or check something for precise use

celestial (suh-LES-chuhl): objects in the day or night sky

contrast (KON-trast): the difference between the dark and light areas of a photograph

diffuse (dih-FYOOZ): to scatter or spread out light

elements (EL-uh-ments): any of more than 100 basic chemical substances that consist of atoms of only one kind

exposure (ik-SPOH-zher): the image resulting from the effect of light on film or a camera's sensor

increments (IN-kruh-ments): a small amount by which something is made larger or greater

optics (OP-tiks): the science that studies light and its effects

resolution (rez-uh-LOO-shun): the sharpness of a photograph or image

sensitivity (sen-si-TIV-eh-tee): the state or quality of being sensitive

sensor (SEN-sawr): a device that detects heat, light, sound, or motion

shutter (SHUHT-er): the device in a camera that limits the passage of light

telephoto (TEL-uh-foh-toh): a lens designed to give a large image of a distant subject

wavelengths (WEYV-lengkths): the distance in the forward motion of a wave from any one point to the next point

Index

cinematography 34
commercial photography 11, 12, 13, 14, 15
developers 36
digital 9, 26, 27, 33, 35, 36, 39
equipment 12, 13, 15, 17, 19, 24, 25, 27
lenses 4, 19, 24, 27, 29, 41, 42
light 5, 7, 8, 10, 17, 19, 20, 33, 34
lighting 4, 12, 31, 32, 33, 34
NASA 18, 19, 21, 22, 23, 25
photojournalists 6, 7, 9, 10, 12
video 17, 35
wavelengths 19, 22

Show What You Know

1. What does STEAM stand for?
2. What STEAM job requires a knowledge of astronomy?
3. How is a camera's lens similar to the human eye?
4. What is the rule of thirds?
5. How can engineers help photographers?

Websites to Visit

http://STEAMjobs.com/filmmakers-photographers-take-math-seriously/
www.nasa.gov
www.digital-photography-school.com

About the Author

Ray Reyes is a freelance photographer and former newspaper reporter. He specializes in photographing weddings, portraits, and events. Ray began taking photos in middle school, and has always loved how photography blends art, science, and technology. In his free time, he enjoys reading, spending time with family and friends, traveling, and binge-watching television shows.

Meet The Author!
www.meetREMauthors.com

© 2017 Rourke Educational Media

All rights reserved. No part of this book may be reproduced or utilized in any form or by any means, electronic or mechanical including photocopying, recording, or by any information storage and retrieval system without permission in writing from the publisher.

www.rourkeeducationalmedia.com

PHOTO CREDITS: Cover images: male photographer © Felix Mizioznikov, female photographer © ChameleonsEye, water splash © Olga Nikonova; page 4-5 © Aphelleon, page 4 football © Herbert Kratky, camera man © Alexander Kirch; page 6-7 © Volodymyr Burdiak, page 7 © wawritto; page 8 right © Anemone, left © Stefano Garau, page 9 bottom © StudioSmart, top © Fabio Lamanna; page 10 © l i g h t p o e t, page 11 © GildaF; page 12-13 © Dean Drobot, page 13 © Nadya Lukic; page 14 © Pir6mon, page 15 © Vladimir Nenezic; page 16 © Monkey Business Images, page 17 top © Peteri, bottom © scyther5; page 18-19 © Radoslaw Lecyk, page 18 Mars © NASA, Pluto mountains © NASA-JHUAPL-SwRI; page 20 © bjonesphotography, page 21 © NASA; page 22 © NASA Ames/JPL-Caltech/T Pyle, page 22-23 © NASA; page 24-25 © fenkieandreas, page 24 © Stefano Garau; page 26 © Volkova Vera, camera © Kletr, page 27 top © Vitaliy Mateha, bottom © nevodka; page 28 © Warongdech (Canon), WHITE RABBIT83; page 30 and 31 © Pavel L Photo and Video; page 32 © Twin Design, page 33 © Joseph Sohm; page 34 -35 © wavebreakmedia, page 35 inset on screen © Mayqel; page 36-37 © scyther5; page 38 © veronicagomezpola, page 39 © Andrey_Popov; page 40 © Matthew (WMF), page 41 © vectorfusionart; page 42 © Goodluz, page 43 © aabeele. All photos from Shutterstock.com except pages 14, 18 (planet surface photos, 21, 22, 23, and 40

Edited by: Keli Sipperley

Cover and Interior design by: Nicola Stratford   www.nicolastratford.com

Library of Congress PCN Data

STEAM Jobs in Photography / Ray Reyes
(STEAM Jobs You'll Love)
ISBN 978-1-68191-743-6 (hard cover)
ISBN 978-1-68191-844-0 (soft cover)
ISBN 978-1-68191-936-2 (e-Book)
Library of Congress Control Number: 2016932706

Printed in the United States of America, North Mankato, Minnesota

Also Available as:
Rourke's e-Books